Valiant Japanese Language School

SUPER REAL JAPANESE

Not in textbooks!

KADOKAWA

Prologue

This book introduces the Japanese language used in casual and real-life situations amongst friends.
For example, young Japanese people would use words such as the following when they encounter a funny situation.

e.g. ウケる。Ukeru

This is a very commonly used expression. However, many people reading this book may be seeing it or hearing it for the first time.

Just like this, there are many expressions that are not taught in Japanese textbooks but are used by young Japanese people.

This is a complete book of such expressions heard by the natives.

We hope that by using this book, you can speak "Natural Japanese".

Downloading Audio Files

This book comes with recordings of a native Japanese speaker reading out the expressions plus the English voice. Please pay attention to the warning notes and proceed to download for free from the link below:

https://www.kadokawa.co.jp/product/321904000764

By accessing the URL above, you can download the ".mp3" format audio files. Please press the download button for "SUPER REAL JAPANESE".

You can also use the app "abceed" and play the audio on your smart phone. abceed is an app you can use to listen to book audio on your smartphone.

 https://www.abceed.com

For details, please access the URL above (Please be aware that depending on the model you are using, it may not be available).

Notes

- ☐ Audio can only be downloaded from a computer (playback is also possible on a smartphone). It cannot be downloaded from mobile phones and smartphones.
- ☐ Audio is saved in mp3 format. To listen, you need a device that can play mp3 files.
- ☐ If you have trouble accessing the download page, please check if your browser is up to date.
- ☐ The folder is compressed, so please decompress before opening and using the file contents.
- ☐ This service may be terminated without notice.

Contents

リアルな感情
Real emotions

リアルな感情

Fun feelings

1. That's hilarious!

2. LMAO.

3. I'm crying.

4. That makes me laugh.

5. It gets funnier and funnier.

6. LMFAO.

7. Seriously funny.

🔊 | 01-01

楽しい
Tanoshī

▸ ▸ ▸ **1.** ウケる。Ukeru

▸ ▸ ▸ **2.** 腹いたい。Hara itai

▸ ▸ ▸ **3.** 涙出てきた。Namida detekita

▸ ▸ ▸ **4.** 笑える。Waraeru

▸ ▸ ▸ **5.** ジワる。Jiwaru

▸ ▸ ▸ **6.** 爆笑。Bakushō

▸ ▸ ▸ **7.** マジ草。Maji kusa

Sad feelings

1. I'm depressed.

2. That's tough.

3. I'm feeling melancholy.

4. I'm disappointed.

5. That's disheartening.

6. I don't feel like doing anything (because I'm so depressed).

7. It makes me cry.

悲しい
Kanashī

▸ ▸ ▸ **1.** 落ちる。Ochiru

▸ ▸ ▸ **2.** つらい。Tsurai

▸ ▸ ▸ **3.** 憂鬱。Yūutsu

▸ ▸ ▸ **4.** がっかりだよ。Gakkari dayo

▸ ▸ ▸ **5.** テンション下がる。Tenshon sagaru

▸ ▸ ▸ **6.** 何も手につかない。Nanimo te ni tsukanai

▸ ▸ ▸ **7.** 泣けてくる。Nakete kuru

リアルな感情

Anger feelings

1. It pisses me off.

2. There's no way.

3. It's annoying.

4. I've reached my limit.

5. I can't do it anymore.

6. Don't mess with me.

7. I snapped.

Real emotions

怒る
Okoru

▸ ▸ ▸ **1.** ムカつく。 Mukatsuku

▸ ▸ ▸ **2.** ありえない。 Arienai

▸ ▸ ▸ **3.** うざい。／うざっ。 Uzai/Uza

▸ ▸ ▸ **4.** もう限界。 Mō genkai

▸ ▸ ▸ **5.** やってらんない。 Yatterannai

▸ ▸ ▸ **6.** ふざけんな。 Fuzakenna

▸ ▸ ▸ **7.** カチンときた。 Kachin to kita

Happy feelings

1. I'm happy (expresses joy). ▸ ▸ ▸

2. Yay! ▸ ▸ ▸

3. I'm psyched! ▸ ▸ ▸

4. I'm happy (expresses contentment). ▸ ▸ ▸

5. I feel fulfilled. ▸ ▸ ▸

6. That's exciting. ▸ ▸ ▸

7. I can't wait! ▸ ▸ ▸

🔊 01-04

喜ぶ
Yorokobu

▸ ▸ ▸ **1.** 嬉しい！ Ureshī

▸ ▸ ▸ **2.** やった！ Yatta

▸ ▸ ▸ **3.** アガる。 Agaru

▸ ▸ ▸ **4.** 幸せ～。 Shiawasē

▸ ▸ ▸ **5.** 満たされるわ。 Mitasareruwa

▸ ▸ ▸ **6.** ワクワク。 Wakuwaku

▸ ▸ ▸ **7.** 楽しみ！ Tanoshimi

Judgement

1. That's amazing. Wow.

2. That's awesome!

3. I like it!

4. It's fine. (not good or bad)

5. It's hard to say.

6. Not bad.

7. That sucks./That's awful.

🔊 01-05

評価
Hyōka

▶ ▶ ▶ **1.** すごい。Sugoi

▶ ▶ ▶ **2.** 最高！Saikō

▶ ▶ ▶ **3.** 気に入った。Kiniitta

▶ ▶ ▶ **4.** 普通。Futsū

▶ ▶ ▶ **5.** 微妙。Bimyō

▶ ▶ ▶ **6.** 悪くない。Warukunai

▶ ▶ ▶ **7.** 最悪。Saiaku

Tiredness

1. I feel lethargic.

2. I'm sleepy.

3. I feel drained.

4. I'm beat.

5. I'm emotionally exhausted.

6. I'm exhausted.

7. I'm dead tired.

Real emotions

疲れ
Tsukare

▸ ▸ ▸ **1.** だるい。Darui

▸ ▸ ▸ **2.** ねみー。／眠い。Nemī/Nemui

▸ ▸ ▸ **3.** へとへと。Hetoheto

▸ ▸ ▸ **4.** ボロボロ。Boroboro

▸ ▸ ▸ **5.** 精神的にくる。Seishin teki ni kuru

▸ ▸ ▸ **6.** くたくた。Kutakuta

▸ ▸ ▸ **7.** 疲れて死にそう。Tsukarete shinisō

リアルな感情

Relaxed feelings

1. I feel calm.

2. It's soothing.

3. to chill out

4. It relaxes me.

5. I feel relieved.

6. to wind down

7. to space out

Real emotions

落ちつく
Ochitsuku

▸ ▸ ▸ **1.** 落ちつく。 Ochitsuku

▸ ▸ ▸ **2.** なごむ。 Nagomu

▸ ▸ ▸ **3.** のんびりする Nombiri suru

▸ ▸ ▸ **4.** 癒される。 Iyasareru

▸ ▸ ▸ **5.** ほっとする。 Hotto suru

▸ ▸ ▸ **6.** ゆっくりする Yukkuri suru

▸ ▸ ▸ **7.** ぼーっとする Bōtto suru

リアルな感情

Being thankful

1. Cheers! ▸ ▸ ▸

2. Thanks! ▸ ▸ ▸

3. It'd help me out. ▸ ▸ ▸

4. I owe you. ▸ ▸ ▸

5. I can always count on you. ▸ ▸ ▸

6. Thanks to ～ . ▸ ▸ ▸

7. I'm grateful. ▸ ▸ ▸

Real emotions

感謝
Kansha

▸ ▸ ▸ **1.** ありがと！ Arigato

▸ ▸ ▸ **2.** サンキュー！ Sankyū

▸ ▸ ▸ **3.** マジ助かる。Maji tasukaru

▸ ▸ ▸ **4.** 恩に着るよ。On ni kiruyo

▸ ▸ ▸ **5.** 頼りになるね。Tayori ni narune

▸ ▸ ▸ **6.** 〜のおかげ！ 〜 no okage

▸ ▸ ▸ **7.** 恐縮っす！ Kyōshuku ssu

Apology

1. I'm very sorry.

2. Sorry!

3. Please forgive me.

4. It won't happen again.

5. I didn't mean it.

6. It's my fault.

7. I've been reflecting on my mistakes.

謝罪
Shazai

▸ ▸ ▸ **1.** ごめん！ Gomen

▸ ▸ ▸ **2.** すまん。 Suman

▸ ▸ ▸ **3.** 許して！ Yurushite

▸ ▸ ▸ **4.** もうしないから。 Mō shinai kara

▸ ▸ ▸ **5.** わざとじゃない。 Wazato janai

▸ ▸ ▸ **6.** 私のせいだよ。 Watashi no sēdayo

▸ ▸ ▸ **7.** 反省してる。 Hansē shiteru

Worried

1. I'm anxious. ▶ ▶ ▶

2. I'm worried. ▶ ▶ ▶

3. I'm nervous. ▶ ▶ ▶

4. to be impatient/to be anxious ▶ ▶ ▶

5. I feel unsettled. ▶ ▶ ▶

6. to have something on one's mind ▶ ▶ ▶

7. I have an upset stomach. ▶ ▶ ▶

🔊 01-10

不安
Fuan

▸ ▸ ▸ **1.** 心配。Shimpai

▸ ▸ ▸ **2.** 不安。Fuan

▸ ▸ ▸ **3.** 緊張する。Kinchō suru

▸ ▸ ▸ **4.** 焦る Aseru

▸ ▸ ▸ **5.** 落ち着かない。Ochitsukanai

▸ ▸ ▸ **6.** 気になる Kininaru

▸ ▸ ▸ **7.** お腹が痛い。Onaka ga itai

Feeling perplexed

1. Huh? ▸ ▸ ▸

2. I don't understand. ▸ ▸ ▸

3. I don't know what to do./
What should I do? ▸ ▸ ▸

4. I have no idea. ▸ ▸ ▸

5. I'm in trouble. ▸ ▸ ▸

6. I'm offended. ▸ ▸ ▸

7. It's a mystery. ▸ ▸ ▸

Real emotions

困惑
Konwaku

▶ ▶ ▶ **1.** は？ Ha

▶ ▶ ▶ **2.** 意味わかんないんだけど。
Imi wakannain dakedo

▶ ▶ ▶ **3.** どうしよう。Dōshiyō

▶ ▶ ▶ **4.** わけわからん。Wake wakaran

▶ ▶ ▶ **5.** 困るよ。Komaruyo

▶ ▶ ▶ **6.** 心外。Shingai

▶ ▶ ▶ **7.** 不思議。Fushigi

リアルな感情

Showing laziness

1. It's troublesome./
   It's a pain in the ass. ▶ ▶ ▶

2. I don't want to do anything. ▶ ▶ ▶

3. I'm bored. ▶ ▶ ▶

4. a lazy person ▶ ▶ ▶

5. I'm unmotivated./
   I can't be bothered. ▶ ▶ ▶

6. to slack off ▶ ▶ ▶

7. to cut corners ▶ ▶ ▶

怠惰
Taida

▸ ▸ ▸ **1.** めんどくさい。Mendokusai

▸ ▸ ▸ **2.** 何もしたくない。Nanimo shitakunai

▸ ▸ ▸ **3.** 退屈。Taikutsu

▸ ▸ ▸ **4.** 怠け者 Namakemono

▸ ▸ ▸ **5.** やる気が出ない。Yaruki ga denai

▸ ▸ ▸ **6.** だらける Darakeru

▸ ▸ ▸ **7.** 手を抜く Te o nuku

Feeling motivated

1. All right.

2. I'm going to do it.

3. to get motivated/ unmotivated

4. I'm getting motivated.

5. I have a feeling I can do it.

6. to get fired up

7. I will do my absolute best.

やる気
Yaruki

▶▶▶ **1.** よーし！ Yōshi

▶▶▶ **2.** やるぞ！ Yaruzo

▶▶▶ **3.** モチベが上がる／下がる
Mochibe ga agaru/sagaru

▶▶▶ **4.** やる気が出てきた。Yaruki ga detekita

▶▶▶ **5.** できる気がする。Dekiru ki ga suru

▶▶▶ **6.** 気合いを入れる Kiai o ireru

▶▶▶ **7.** 一生懸命頑張ります！
Isshōkemmē gambari masu

Feeling impressed

1. I'm moved.

2. I'm blown away.

3. I'm overwhelmed with emotion.

4. I'm touched.

5. It warms my heart.

6. I'm getting emotional./ I'm tearing up.

7. This is an emotional moment.

感動
Kandō

▸ ▸ ▸ **1.** 感動した。Kandō shita

▸ ▸ ▸ **2.** 感激！Kangeki

▸ ▸ ▸ **3.** 胸がいっぱい。Mune ga ippai

▸ ▸ ▸ **4.** ジーンとした。Jīn to shita

▸ ▸ ▸ **5.** しみるわー。Shimiru wā

▸ ▸ ▸ **6.** 泣ける。Nakeru

▸ ▸ ▸ **7.** グッとくる。Gutto kuru

リアルな感情

Sense of shame

1. I'm embarrassed.

2. I'm blushing.

3. I want to dig a hole and hide in it.

4. I feel like running away.

5. I'm ashamed.

6. I can't bear the embarrassment.

7. I'm (a little) shy.

Real emotions

羞恥心
Shūchishin

▶ ▶ ▶ **1.** 恥ずかしい。Hazukashī

▶ ▶ ▶ **2.** 照れるなぁ。Tererunā

▶ ▶ ▶ **3.** 穴があったら入りたい。
Ana ga attara hairitai

▶ ▶ ▶ **4.** 逃げ出したい。Nigedashitai

▶ ▶ ▶ **5.** 情けない。Nasakenai

▶ ▶ ▶ **6.** いたたまれない。Itatamarenai

▶ ▶ ▶ **7.** シャイなんです。Shai nan desu

リアルな会話

Real conversations

Emphasis

1. pretty

2. seriously

3. truly

4. really

5. all jokes aside

6. super

7. quite

強調
Kyōchō

▸ ▸ ▸ **1.** フツーに Futsū ni

▸ ▸ ▸ **2.** マジで Maji de

▸ ▸ ▸ **3.** ガチで Gachi de

▸ ▸ ▸ **4.** リアルに Riaru ni

▸ ▸ ▸ **5.** 冗談抜きに Jōdan nuki ni

▸ ▸ ▸ **6.** 超 Chō

▸ ▸ ▸ **7.** かなり Kanari

Starting a conversation

1. Hey. Hey.

2. Have you heard that?/
Did you hear that?

3. Hey, do you know ~ ? /
Do you know about ~ ?

4. Oh, by the way.

5. Hey, do you have time right
now?

6. Guess what?

7. Oh yeah! ※When you remember
something that you wanted to say

話し始め
Hanashi hajime

▸ ▸ ▸ **1.** ねえねえ。Nē nē

▸ ▸ ▸ **2.** あれ聞いた? Are kiita

▸ ▸ ▸ **3.** ～って知ってる? ～ tte shitteru

▸ ▸ ▸ **4.** そういえばさ。Sōiebasa

▸ ▸ ▸ **5.** 今、大丈夫? 時間ある?
Ima daijōbu Jikan aru

▸ ▸ ▸ **6.** あのさ～。Anosā

▸ ▸ ▸ **7.** あっ! A
※何か言いたいことを思い出したとき

Positive responses

1. Nice! ▸ ▸ ▸

2. It's OK. ▸ ▸ ▸

3. I see. ▸ ▸ ▸

4. That's true./I agree. ▸ ▸ ▸

5. Got it! ▸ ▸ ▸

6. Understood! ▸ ▸ ▸

7. That's right. ▸ ▸ ▸

Real conversations

ポジティブなリアクション
Pojitibuna riakushon

▶ ▶ ▶ **1.** いいね！ Īne

▶ ▶ ▶ **2.** 大丈夫。 Daijōbu

▶ ▶ ▶ **3.** なるほど。 Naruhodo

▶ ▶ ▶ **4.** たしかに。 Tashikani

▶ ▶ ▶ **5.** 了解。／りょ。 Ryōkai/Ryo

▶ ▶ ▶ **6.** わかった。 Wakatta

▶ ▶ ▶ **7.** そうそう。 Sōsō

Negative responses

1. No way.

2. That's crazy.

3. I don't want to.

4. It's not happening.
(I'm not going to do it.)

5. Give me a break!

6. No no no.

7. No kidding!

Real conversations

ネガティブなリアクション
Negatibuna riakushon

▶ ▶ ▶ **1.** ないわ。Naiwa

▶ ▶ ▶ **2.** やばいね。Yabaine

▶ ▶ ▶ **3.** やだ。Yada

▶ ▶ ▶ **4.** マジ無理。Maji muri

▶ ▶ ▶ **5.** 勘弁して。Kamben shite

▶ ▶ ▶ **6.** いやいやいや。Iya iya iya

▶ ▶ ▶ **7.** 冗談でしょ。Jōdan desho

Surprised responses

1. Seriously? ▸ ▸ ▸

2. You scared me! ▸ ▸ ▸

3. That's horrible! ▸ ▸ ▸

4. That turns me off. ▸ ▸ ▸

5. What!? ▸ ▸ ▸

6. Really? ▸ ▸ ▸

7. No way! ▸ ▸ ▸

Real conversations

驚きのリアクション
Odoroki no riakushon

▸▸▸ **1.** マジで？ Maji de

▸▸▸ **2.** ビビるわ！ Bibiruwa

▸▸▸ **3.** エグいな。 Eguina

▸▸▸ **4.** 引くんだけど。 Hikundakedo

▸▸▸ **5.** え〜？　は〜？ Ē Hā

▸▸▸ **6.** うそ！　うそでしょ !?
Uso Uso desho

▸▸▸ **7.** まさか！ Masaka

Conveying discontent

1. I'm fed up.

2. Please explain.

3. What is happening?

4. I'm not satisfied./
I can't accept this.

5. Please do it properly.

6. Please do something about it.

7. to start to dislike

🔊 | 02-06

不満を伝える
Fuman o tsutaeru

▸▸▸ **1.** うんざりです。Unzari desu

▸▸▸ **2.** ちゃんと説明してください。
Chanto setsumē shitekudasai

▸▸▸ **3.** どうなってるんですか。
Dōnatterun desuka

▸▸▸ **4.** 納得できません。Nattoku dekimasen

▸▸▸ **5.** ちゃんとやってください。
Chanto yatte kudasai

▸▸▸ **6.** なんとかしてください。
Nantoka shitekudasai

▸▸▸ **7.** 嫌になる Iya ni naru

Thoughtfulness

1. Don't overdo it.

2. Take care of yourself.

3. Get better soon.

4. Don't push yourself too hard.

5. Rest up.

6. Thanks for your hard work.

7. Take care.

思いやりの表現
Omoiyari no hyōgen

▶ ▶ ▶ **1.** 無理しないでね。Muri shinaidene

▶ ▶ ▶ **2.** お大事に。Odaijini

▶ ▶ ▶ **3.** 早く良くなってね。
Hayaku yokunattene

▶ ▶ ▶ **4.** 頑張りすぎないで。Gambarisuginaide

▶ ▶ ▶ **5.** ゆっくり休んでね。
Yukkuri yasundene

▶ ▶ ▶ **6.** お疲れさま！Otsukaresama

▶ ▶ ▶ **7.** 気をつけてね。Ki o tsuketene

Stimulating conversation

1. And what happened after that?

2. Such as?

3. What do you mean?

4. What? That's hilarious.

5. Tell me more.

6. Why?

7. But…

話を広げる
Hanashi o hirogeru

▸ ▸ ▸ **1.** それで、それで？ Sorede, sorede

▸ ▸ ▸ **2.** たとえば？ Tatoeba

▸ ▸ ▸ **3.** どゆこと？ Doyukoto

▸ ▸ ▸ **4.** 何それ、ウケるんだけど。
Nani sore, ukerundakedo

▸ ▸ ▸ **5.** 詳しく教えて！ Kuwashiku oshiete

▸ ▸ ▸ **6.** 何で!? Nande

▸ ▸ ▸ **7.** でもさ…… Demosa

Rephrasing

1. for example   ▸ ▸ ▸

2. in other words   ▸ ▸ ▸

3. put simply   ▸ ▸ ▸

4. that means   ▸ ▸ ▸

5. in short   ▸ ▸ ▸

6. to summarize   ▸ ▸ ▸

7. roughly speaking   ▸ ▸ ▸

言い換える
Īkaeru

▸ ▸ ▸ **1.** たとえば Tatoeba

▸ ▸ ▸ **2.** つまりさ Tsumarisa

▸ ▸ ▸ **3.** わかりやすく言うと
Wakariyasuku iuto

▸ ▸ ▸ **4.** ということは To iukotowa

▸ ▸ ▸ **5.** 要は Yōwa

▸ ▸ ▸ **6.** まとめると Matomeruto

▸ ▸ ▸ **7.** ざっくり言うと Zakkuri iuto

Praise

1. I knew you could do it.

2. You're so thoughtful.

3. It looks good on you.

4. How did you know that?

5. You're a genius.

6. I respect you.

7. You have good taste.

褒め言葉
Homekotoba

▸ ▸ ▸ **1.** さすが。 Sasuga

▸ ▸ ▸ **2.** 優しい。 Yasashī

▸ ▸ ▸ **3.** それ似合ってるね。 Sore niatterune

▸ ▸ ▸ **4.** よくわかったね。 Yoku wakattane

▸ ▸ ▸ **5.** 天才。 Tensai

▸ ▸ ▸ **6.** 尊敬するよ。 Sonkē suruyo

▸ ▸ ▸ **7.** センスいいね。 Sensu īne

Humbleness

1. I have still got a long way to go.

2. I didn't know.

3. I can learn a lot from you.

4. I want to follow your example.

5. That's not true.

6. I know it's just flattery, but I appreciate it.

7. Don't mention it.

🔊 02-11

謙遜
Kenson

▸ ▸ ▸ **1.** まだまだです。Madamada desu

▸ ▸ ▸ **2.** 知らなかった！Shiranakatta

▸ ▸ ▸ **3.** 勉強になります。
Benkyō ni narimasu

▸ ▸ ▸ **4.** 見習いたい。Minaraitai

▸ ▸ ▸ **5.** そんなことないよ。Sonna koto naiyo

▸ ▸ ▸ **6.** お世辞でも嬉しいです。
Oseji demo ureshī desu

▸ ▸ ▸ **7.** とんでもない。Tondemonai

Encouragement

1. Do your best./Good luck. ▸ ▸ ▸

2. Cheer up. ▸ ▸ ▸

3. You can do it. ▸ ▸ ▸

4. Don't give up. ▸ ▸ ▸

5. Everything will be fine. ▸ ▸ ▸

6. Believe in yourself. ▸ ▸ ▸

7. Be confident. ▸ ▸ ▸

励まし
Hagemashi

▸ ▸ ▸ **1.** 頑張って！ Gambatte

▸ ▸ ▸ **2.** 元気出して。 Genki dashite

▸ ▸ ▸ **3.** あなたならできるよ。
Anata nara dekiruyo

▸ ▸ ▸ **4.** 諦めないで。 Akiramenaide

▸ ▸ ▸ **5.** きっとうまくいくよ。 Kitto umaku ikuyo

▸ ▸ ▸ **6.** 自分を信じて。 Jibun o shinjite

▸ ▸ ▸ **7.** 自信持って。 Jishin motte

Beauty

1. I got fat again.

2. I want to lose some weight.

3. The meat around my belly bothers me.

4. I need to go on a diet.

5. I don't want to get tanned.

6. I got a pimple.

7. I want to get hair removal.

美容
Biyō

▶ ▶ ▶ **1.** また太っちゃった。Mata futocchatta

▶ ▶ ▶ **2.** 痩せたいなぁ。Yasetainā

▶ ▶ ▶ **3.** お腹のお肉が気になる。
Onaka no oniku ga kininaru

▶ ▶ ▶ **4.** ダイエットしなきゃ。Daietto shinakya

▶ ▶ ▶ **5.** 日焼けしたくない。Hiyake shitakunai

▶ ▶ ▶ **6.** ニキビができちゃった。
Nikibi ga dekichatta

▶ ▶ ▶ **7.** 脱毛したい。Datsumō shitai

Changing the topic

1. by the way ▸ ▸ ▸

2. I'm changing the subject, but ▸ ▸ ▸

3. more importantly ▸ ▸ ▸

4. Let's put that aside. ▸ ▸ ▸

5. incidentally ▸ ▸ ▸

6. anyway/In any case ▸ ▸ ▸

7. speaking of ～ ▸ ▸ ▸

話題を変える
Wadai o kaeru

▶ ▶ ▶ **1.** てかさ Tekasa

▶ ▶ ▶ **2.** 話変わるけど、Hanashi kawarukedo

▶ ▶ ▶ **3.** そんなことより Sonna kotoyori

▶ ▶ ▶ **4.** それはそうと Sorewa sōto

▶ ▶ ▶ **5.** ところで Tokorode

▶ ▶ ▶ **6.** とにかく Tonikaku

▶ ▶ ▶ **7.** 〜といえば To ieba

Accepting an invitation

1. Sounds good.

2. I want to go.

3. Sure.

4. I'd love to.

5. Yes, I'm available.

6. Yes, I am free.

7. I'd be glad to.

誘いを受ける
Sasoi o ukeru

▶ ▶ ▶ **1.** いいねー。Īnē

▶ ▶ ▶ **2.** 行きたい！Ikitai

▶ ▶ ▶ **3.** もちろん。Mochiron

▶ ▶ ▶ **4.** ぜひ！Zehi

▶ ▶ ▶ **5.** うん、空いてるよ。Un, aiteru yo

▶ ▶ ▶ **6.** うん、暇だよ。Un, hima dayo

▶ ▶ ▶ **7.** 喜んで。Yorokonde

Declining an invitation

1. That day is a little difficult.

2. I'm not available.

3. I have other plans.

4. I would have loved to go.

5. Maybe next time.

6. Please invite me again.

7. Let me check my plans.

Real conversations

誘いを断る
Sasoi o kotowaru

▸ ▸ ▸ **1.** その日はちょっと……。
Sono hi wa chotto

▸ ▸ ▸ **2.** 都合が悪いんだ。Tsugō ga waruinda

▸ ▸ ▸ **3.** 他に約束があるんだ。
Hoka ni yakusoku ga arunda

▸ ▸ ▸ **4.** 行きたかった。Ikitakatta

▸ ▸ ▸ **5.** またの機会に。Matano kikai ni

▸ ▸ ▸ **6.** また誘ってー。Mata sasottē

▸ ▸ ▸ **7.** 予定確認させて。Yotē kakunin sasete

Words that connect sentences

1. conversely

2. after all

3. actually/sure enough

4. despite/even though

5. moreover/besides

6. that's why/so

7. and then/after that

🔊 02-17

文章をつなぐ言葉
Bunshō o tsunagu kotoba

▸ ▸ ▸ **1.** 逆に Gyakuni

▸ ▸ ▸ **2.** 結局 Kekkyoku

▸ ▸ ▸ **3.** やっぱり Yappari

▸ ▸ ▸ **4.** なのに Nanoni

▸ ▸ ▸ **5.** しかも Shikamo

▸ ▸ ▸ **6.** だから Dakara

▸ ▸ ▸ **7.** それから Sorekara

Vague time words

1. occasionally

2. always

3. sometimes

4. recently

5. just now

6. for a long time/for ages

7. forever

微妙な時間
Bimyōna jikan

▸ ▸ ▸ **1.** たまに Tamani

▸ ▸ ▸ **2.** いつも Itsumo

▸ ▸ ▸ **3.** 時々 Tokidoki

▸ ▸ ▸ **4.** この頃 Konogoro

▸ ▸ ▸ **5.** さっき Sakki

▸ ▸ ▸ **6.** ずっと Zutto

▸ ▸ ▸ **7.** いつまでも Itsumademo

リアルな1日

Real life routine

Casual greeting

1. Hello.

2. Good evening.

3. Hi there.

4. Hey.

5. Hi.

6. Yo.

7. (Showing gratitude towards colleagues, teammates)

気軽な挨拶
Kigaruna aisatsu

▸ ▸ ▸ **1.** こんにちは。 Konnichiwa

▸ ▸ ▸ **2.** こんばんは。 Kombanwa

▸ ▸ ▸ **3.** どうも。 Dōmo

▸ ▸ ▸ **4.** うっす。 Ussu

▸ ▸ ▸ **5.** ちわ。 Chiwa

▸ ▸ ▸ **6.** よう。 Yō

▸ ▸ ▸ **7.** おつかれっす。 Otsukare ssu

Commuting to work or school

1. to oversleep

2. to be half asleep

3. to eat breakfast

4. to put on make-up

5. to get on a full train

6. The train is running late.

7. to be just in time

朝〜通勤・通学
Asa 〜 Tsūkin, Tsūgaku

▶ ▶ ▶ **1.** 寝坊する　Nebō suru

▶ ▶ ▶ **2.** 寝ぼける　Nebokeru

▶ ▶ ▶ **3.** 朝ごはんを食べる
Asagohan o taberu

▶ ▶ ▶ **4.** メイクする　Meiku suru

▶ ▶ ▶ **5.** 満員電車に乗る
Man-indensha ni noru

▶ ▶ ▶ **6.** 電車が遅れてる。
Densha ga okureteru

▶ ▶ ▶ **7.** ギリギリ間に合う　Girigiri maniau

Work

1. to skip work

2. to focus on work

3. to attend a meeting

4. to make a mistake at work

5. to take a coffee/tea/smoking break

6. to be scolded by the boss

7. to complain

Real life routine

仕事
Shigoto

▸ ▸ ▸ **1.** 仕事をサボる　Shigoto o saboru

▸ ▸ ▸ **2.** 仕事に集中する
Shigoto ni shūchū suru

▸ ▸ ▸ **3.** 会議に参加する　Kaigi ni sanka suru

▸ ▸ ▸ **4.** 仕事でミスる　Shigoto de misuru

▸ ▸ ▸ **5.** 一服する　Ippuku suru

▸ ▸ ▸ **6.** 上司に怒られる
Jōshi ni okorareru

▸ ▸ ▸ **7.** 愚痴る　Guchiru

At night

1. to work overtime ▸ ▸

2. to go for a drink ▸ ▸

3. to go somewhere and then go straight home ▸ ▸

4. to stop by the supermarket ▸ ▸

5. to drink at home ▸ ▸

6. to play with a pet ▸ ▸ ▸

7. to fall asleep ▸ ▸ ▸

夜
Yoru

▸ ▸ ▸ **1.** 残業する　Zangyō suru

▸ ▸ ▸ **2.** 一杯飲みに行く　Ippai nomini iku

▸ ▸ ▸ **3.** 直行直帰する　Chokkō chokki suru

▸ ▸ ▸ **4.** スーパーに寄る　Sūpā ni yoru

▸ ▸ ▸ **5.** 家飲みする　Ienomi suru

▸ ▸ ▸ **6.** ペットと遊ぶ　Petto to asobu

▸ ▸ ▸ **7.** 寝落ちする　Neochi suru

リアルな1日

Before going to bed

1. to take off one's make-up › › ›

2. to do skincare › › ›

3. to meditate › › ›

4. to brush one's teeth › › ›

5. to take a bath › › ›

6. to give oneself a massage › › ›

7. to get into bed › › ›

Real life routine

寝る前
Nerumae

▸ ▸ ▸ **1.** メイクを落とす Meiku o otosu

▸ ▸ ▸ **2.** スキンケアする Sukinkea suru

▸ ▸ ▸ **3.** 瞑想する Mēsō suru

▸ ▸ ▸ **4.** 歯磨きする Hamigaki suru

▸ ▸ ▸ **5.** お風呂に入る Ofuro ni hairu

▸ ▸ ▸ **6.** マッサージする Massāji suru

▸ ▸ ▸ **7.** ベッドに入る Beddo ni hairu

Going out on a day off

1. to chat at a family restaurant ▸ ▸

2. to walk around downtown ▸ ▸

3. to have tea ▸ ▸

4. to have lunch ▸ ▸

5. to go to a large public bath ▸ ▸

6. to go for karaoke ▸ ▸

7. to go for a drive ▸ ▸

Real life routine

休日に外へ行く
Kyūjitsu ni soto e iku

▸ ▸ ▸ **1.** ファミレスでダべる
Famiresu de daberu

▸ ▸ ▸ **2.** 街ブラする　Machibura suru

▸ ▸ ▸ **3.** お茶する　Ocha suru

▸ ▸ ▸ **4.** ランチする　Ranchi suru

▸ ▸ ▸ **5.** スーパー銭湯に行く
Sūpāsentō ni iku

▸ ▸ ▸ **6.** カラオケに行く　Karaoke ni iku

▸ ▸ ▸ **7.** ドライブする　Doraibu suru

Chilling at home on a day off

1. to be lazy

2. to chill out

3. to shut oneself inside

4. to watch Netflix

5. to serve one's home cooking to someone

6. to click the buy button on an EC site

7. to get a ton of sleep

休日にお家で過ごす
Kyūjitsu ni ouchi de sugosu

▶ ▶ ▶ **1.** だらだらする　Daradara suru

▶ ▶ ▶ **2.** まったりする　Mattari suru

▶ ▶ ▶ **3.** 引きこもる　Hikikomoru

▶ ▶ ▶ **4.** ネトフリ見る　Netofuri miru

▶ ▶ ▶ **5.** 手料理を振る舞う
Teryōri o furumau

▶ ▶ ▶ **6.** ECサイトでポチる
Īshī saito de pochiru

▶ ▶ ▶ **7.** 寝まくる　Nemakuru

House chores

1. to do cleaning

2. to do the laundry

3. to take out the trash

4. to prepare dinner

5. to do the vacuuming

6. to iron one's clothes

7. to take (a garment) to the dry cleaners

Real life routine

家事
Kaji

▶ ▶ ▶ **1.** 掃除する Sōji suru

▶ ▶ ▶ **2.** 洗濯する Sentaku suru

▶ ▶ ▶ **3.** ゴミを捨てる Gomi o suteru

▶ ▶ ▶ **4.** 夕飯の用意をする
Yūhan no yōi o suru

▶ ▶ ▶ **5.** 掃除機をかける Sōjiki o kakeru

▶ ▶ ▶ **6.** アイロンをかける Airon o kakeru

▶ ▶ ▶ **7.** クリーニングに出す
Kurīningu ni dasu

Exercise

1. to go to the gym　▷ ▷ ▷

2. to go jogging　▷ ▷ ▷

3. to stretch　▷ ▷ ▷

4. to do yoga　▷ ▷ ▷

5. to work out　▷ ▷ ▷

6. to increase one's physical strength　▷ ▷ ▷

7. to tighten around the waist　▷ ▷ ▷

🔊 | 03-09

運動
Undō

▸ ▸ ▸ **1.** ジムに行く　Jimu ni iku

▸ ▸ ▸ **2.** ジョギングする　Jogingu suru

▸ ▸ ▸ **3.** ストレッチする　Sutorecchi suru

▸ ▸ ▸ **4.** ヨガする　Yoga suru

▸ ▸ ▸ **5.** 筋トレする　Kintore suru

▸ ▸ ▸ **6.** 体力をつける　Tairyoku o tsukeru

▸ ▸ ▸ **7.** お腹を引き締める
Onaka o hikishimeru

Hairdresser's

1. Could you give me this style (while pointing at the picture)?

2. Please shorten it by about 2 cm.

3. I want to grow it.

4. Please don't cut it here.

5. Please dye my hair.

6. This is just fine.

7. Just a trim, please.

美容院
Biyōin

▸▸▸ **1.** この写真みたいにしてください。
Kono shashin mitaini shite kudasai

▸▸▸ **2.** 2cmくらい短くしてください。
Ni senchi kurai mijikaku shite kudasai

▸▸▸ **3.** 伸ばしたいです。Nobashitai desu

▸▸▸ **4.** ここは切らないでください。
Koko wa kiranaide kudasai

▸▸▸ **5.** 染めてください。Somete kudasai

▸▸▸ **6.** ちょうどいいです。Chōdo īdesu

▸▸▸ **7.** 毛先を揃える程度にしてください。
Kesaki o soroeru tēdo ni shite kudasai

Everyday shopping

1. to buy extra things

2. to only buy what one needs

3. to buy groceries

4. to accumulate points

5. to use points

6. to use the self-checkout

7. to run out of toilet paper

🔊 03-11

日々の買い物
Hibi no kaimono

▶ ▶ ▶ **1.** 余分なものを買う
Yobun na mono o kau

▶ ▶ ▶ **2.** 必要なものだけ買う
Hitsuyōna monodake kau

▶ ▶ ▶ **3.** 日用品を買う　Nichiyōhin o kau

▶ ▶ ▶ **4.** ポイントを貯める　Pointo o tameru

▶ ▶ ▶ **5.** ポイントを使う　Pointo o tsukau

▶ ▶ ▶ **6.** セルフレジで買う　Serufureji de kau

▶ ▶ ▶ **7.** トイレットペーパーを切らす
Toirettopēpā o kirasu

Work style

1. to work as a full-time employee

2. to work part-time

3. to work as a freelancer

4. to have a side job

5. working from home

6. to quit a job

7. to change jobs

働き方
Hatarakikata

▸▸▸ **1.** 正社員として働く
Sēshain toshite hataraku

▸▸▸ **2.** アルバイトをする　Arubaito o suru

▸▸▸ **3.** フリーランスで働く
Furīransu de hataraku

▸▸▸ **4.** 副業をする　Fukugyō o suru

▸▸▸ **5.** 在宅ワーク　Zaitaku wāku

▸▸▸ **6.** 仕事を辞める　Shigoto o yameru

▸▸▸ **7.** 転職する　Tenshoku suru

Plans

1. to make plans

2. to reschedule

3. to arrange to meet somewhere

4. to get some extra work

5. to already have plans/to have a previous engagement

6. to meet up

7. to cancel at the last minute

予定
Yotē

▶ ▶ ▶ **1.** 予定を立てる　Yotē o tateru

▶ ▶ ▶ **2.** リスケする　Risuke suru

▶ ▶ ▶ **3.** 待ち合わせを決める
Machiawase o kimeru

▶ ▶ ▶ **4.** 別の仕事が入る
Betsu no shigoto ga hairu

▶ ▶ ▶ **5.** 先約がある　Senyaku ga aru

▶ ▶ ▶ **6.** 集合する　Shūgō suru

▶ ▶ ▶ **7.** ドタキャンする　Dotakyan suru

Weather condition

1. It looks like it's gonna rain.

2. It's getting cloudy.

3. I think you should take an umbrella.

4. It's a beautiful day.

5. A typhoon is coming.

6. I wonder if it will be sunny tomorrow.

7. It's getting warmer recently, isn't it?

天気
Tenki

▶ ▶ ▶ **1.** 雨が降りそう。Ame ga furisō

▶ ▶ ▶ **2.** 曇ってきた。Kumottekita

▶ ▶ ▶ **3.** 傘持って行った方がいいよ。
Kasa motteitta hōga īyo

▶ ▶ ▶ **4.** いい天気だね。Ītenki dane

▶ ▶ ▶ **5.** 台風が来るよ。Taifū ga kuruyo

▶ ▶ ▶ **6.** 明日晴れるかなぁ。
Ashita harerukanā

▶ ▶ ▶ **7.** 最近暖かくなってきたね。
Saikin atatakakunattekitane

Talking about money

1. to save up   ▸ ▸ ▸

2. to splurge on unnecessary things   ▸ ▸ ▸

3. to treat someone   ▸ ▸ ▸

4. to split the bill   ▸ ▸ ▸

5. to pay separately   ▸ ▸ ▸

6. to get a receipt   ▸ ▸ ▸

7. to borrow money   ▸ ▸ ▸

お金について話す
Okane ni tsuite hanasu

▸ ▸ ▸ **1.** 貯金する Chokin suru

▸ ▸ ▸ **2.** 無駄遣いする Mudazukai suru

▸ ▸ ▸ **3.** 奢る Ogoru

▸ ▸ ▸ **4.** 割り勘にする Warikan ni suru

▸ ▸ ▸ **5.** 別々に払う Betsubetsu ni harau

▸ ▸ ▸ **6.** 領収書をもらう Ryōshūsho o morau

▸ ▸ ▸ **7.** お金を借りる Okane o kariru

Useful phrases and messages

1. What are you doing right now? ▸ ▸ ▸

2. Are you free tomorrow? ▸ ▸ ▸

3. When is good for you? ▸ ▸ ▸

4. Where should we meet? ▸ ▸ ▸

5. I'll be there soon. ▸ ▸ ▸

6. I'm on my way. ▸ ▸ ▸

7. I'll be 10 minutes late. ▸ ▸ ▸

便利なフレーズ・メッセージ
Benri na furēzu, messēji

▸ ▸ ▸ **1.** 今何してる？ Ima nani shiteru

▸ ▸ ▸ **2.** 明日、ひま？ Ashita hima

▸ ▸ ▸ **3.** いつがいい？ Itsu ga ī

▸ ▸ ▸ **4.** どこにする？ Doko ni suru

▸ ▸ ▸ **5.** もうすぐ着くよ。 Mōsugu tsuku yo

▸ ▸ ▸ **6.** 今向かってる。 Ima mukatteru

▸ ▸ ▸ **7.** 10分遅れる。 Juppun okureru

Trouble on the train

1. to miss the last train ▸ ▸ ▸

2. to miss the train ▸ ▸ ▸

3. to go past one's stop ▸ ▸ ▸

4. The train is delayed. ▸ ▸ ▸

5. to take the wrong train ▸ ▸ ▸

6. to get a certificate of delay ▸ ▸

7. to fall asleep and miss one's stop ▸ ▸ ▸

🔊 | 03-17

電車のトラブル
Densha no toraburu

▸ ▸ ▸ **1.** 終電を逃す　Shūden o nogasu

▸ ▸ ▸ **2.** 電車に乗り遅れる
Densha ni noriokureru

▸ ▸ ▸ **3.** 乗り過ごす　Norisugosu

▸ ▸ ▸ **4.** 電車が遅れている。
Densha ga okureteiru

▸ ▸ ▸ **5.** 電車を間違える
Densha o machigaeru

▸ ▸ ▸ **6.** 遅延証明書をもらう
Chien shōmēsho o morau

▸ ▸ ▸ **7.** 寝過ごす　Nesugosu

リアルな食事

Real dining

リアルな食事

Good reaction

1. Delicious.

2. Yummy.

3. Can't get enough of it!

4. It melts in one's mouth.

5. Super delicious.

6. I'm craving some rice.

7. I can eat this endlessly.

おいしい
Oishī

▸ ▸ ▸ **1.** おいしい。Oishī

▸ ▸ ▸ **2.** うまい。Umai

▸ ▸ ▸ **3.** たまんないわ。Tamannaiwa

▸ ▸ ▸ **4.** とろける。Torokeru

▸ ▸ ▸ **5.** 激うま。Geki uma

▸ ▸ ▸ **6.** ご飯がほしくなる。
Gohan ga hoshikunaru

▸ ▸ ▸ **7.** いくらでも食べられる。
Ikurademo taberareru

Taste 1

1. sweet

2. bitter

3. spicy

4. salty

5. refreshing

6. greasy/fatty/oily

7. rich in flavor

味 1
Aji 1

▸ ▸ ▸ **1.** 甘い Amai

▸ ▸ ▸ **2.** 苦い Nigai

▸ ▸ ▸ **3.** 辛い Karai

▸ ▸ ▸ **4.** しょっぱい Shoppai

▸ ▸ ▸ **5.** さっぱりしてる Sappari shiteru

▸ ▸ ▸ **6.** 脂っこい Aburakkoi

▸ ▸ ▸ **7.** コクがある Koku ga aru

Taste II

1. sweet and spicy

2. watery

3. weak flavored

4. addictive

5. sour

6. hot in the nose (like wasabi)

7. bitter/astringent (like green tea)

味2
Aji 2

▶ ▶ ▶ **1.** 甘辛い Amakarai

▶ ▶ ▶ **2.** 水っぽい Mizuppoi

▶ ▶ ▶ **3.** 薄味 Usuaji

▶ ▶ ▶ **4.** クセになる Kuse ni naru

▶ ▶ ▶ **5.** 酸っぱい Suppai

▶ ▶ ▶ **6.** ツーンとする ※わさびなどの味。
Tsūn to suru

▶ ▶ ▶ **7.** 渋い ※お茶など。 Shibui

Food texture

1. doughy/elastic

2. fluffy

3. syrupy/pulpy

4. crunchy

5. crispy (fried food)

6. crispy (fresh vegetables)

7. sticky

食感
Shokkan

▸ ▸ ▸ **1.** もちもち Mochimochi

▸ ▸ ▸ **2.** ふわふわ Fuwafuwa

▸ ▸ ▸ **3.** トロトロ Torotoro

▸ ▸ ▸ **4.** カリカリ Karikari

▸ ▸ ▸ **5.** サクサク Sakusaku

▸ ▸ ▸ **6.** シャキシャキ Shakishaki

▸ ▸ ▸ **7.** ネバネバ Nebaneba

Describing temperature of things

1. soft and fluffy (like baked sweet potatoes) ▸ ▸ ▸

2. burning hot (like curry or steak) ▸ ▸ ▸

3. cool and pleasant (like ice cream or juice) ▸ ▸ ▸

4. (got) cold (like soup) ▸ ▸ ▸

5. ice-cold (like beer) ▸ ▸ ▸

6. lukewarm (like beer) ▸ ▸ ▸

7. warm (like soup) ▸ ▸ ▸

温度感
Ondokan

▶ ▶ ▶ **1.** ほくほく ※焼き芋など。Hokuhoku

▶ ▶ ▶ **2.** アツアツ ※カレー、ステーキなど。
Atsuatsu

▶ ▶ ▶ **3.** ひんやり ※アイス、ジュースなど。
Hinyari

▶ ▶ ▶ **4.** 冷めた ※スープなど。Sameta

▶ ▶ ▶ **5.** キンキン ※ビールなど。Kinkin

▶ ▶ ▶ **6.** 生ぬるい ※ビールなど。Namanurui

▶ ▶ ▶ **7.** あったかい ※スープなど。Attakai

Cooking a meal

1. to wash rice

2. to steam rice

3. to fry tempura

4. to change the taste

5. to put in the microwave

6. to prepare a meal with various leftovers

7. to put time and effort into cooking

食事を作る
Shokuji o tsukuru

▸ ▸ ▸ **1.** お米をとぐ Okome o togu

▸ ▸ ▸ **2.** ご飯を炊く Gohan o taku

▸ ▸ ▸ **3.** てんぷらを揚げる Tempura o ageru

▸ ▸ ▸ **4.** 味変する Ajihen suru

▸ ▸ ▸ **5.** レンチンする Renchin suru

▸ ▸ ▸ **6.** あり合わせで作る
Ariawase de tsukuru

▸ ▸ ▸ **7.** 手間暇かける Temahima kakeru

リアルな食事

Eating

1. to eat out

2. to get takeout

3. to try/taste (food)

4. to pick at something before the meal is ready or before other people are ready to start it

5. to order in

6. to have a midnight snack

7. to eat while walking around

食事
Shokuji

▸ ▸ ▸ **1.** 外食する Gaishoku suru

▸ ▸ ▸ **2.** テイクアウトする Teikuauto suru

▸ ▸ ▸ **3.** 味見する Ajimi suru

▸ ▸ ▸ **4.** つまみ食いする Tsumamigui suru

▸ ▸ ▸ **5.** 出前をとる Demae o toru

▸ ▸ ▸ **6.** 夜食を食べる Yashoku o taberu

▸ ▸ ▸ **7.** 食べ歩きする Tabearuki suru

Going out for food/drinks

1. to bar-hop

2. to go to an afterparty

3. to go to one of one's favorite bars/restaurants

4. to explore/discover new bars/restaurants

5. to café-hop

6. to order all-you-can-drink

7. free refills

外食のフレーズ
Gaishoku no furēzu

▶ ▶ ▶ **1.** はしごする　Hashigo suru

▶ ▶ ▶ **2.** 二次会に行く　Nijikai ni iku

▶ ▶ ▶ **3.** 行きつけの店に行く
Ikitsuke no mise ni iku

▶ ▶ ▶ **4.** 新しい店を開拓する
Atarashī mise o kaitaku suru

▶ ▶ ▶ **5.** カフェ巡りをする　Kafe meguri o suru

▶ ▶ ▶ **6.** 飲み放題を頼む　Nomihōdai o tanomu

▶ ▶ ▶ **7.** おかわり自由　Okawari jiyū

Feeling hungry

1. I'm hungry.

2. I'm starving.

3. I'm full.

4. to eat until 80 percent full

5. I'm thirsty.

6. I have a craving for chocolate.

7. I always have room for dessert.

Real dining

食欲
Shokuyoku

▸ ▸ ▸ **1.** お腹が空いた。Onaka ga suita

▸ ▸ ▸ **2.** お腹ぺこぺこ。Onaka pekopeko

▸ ▸ ▸ **3.** お腹いっぱい。Onaka ippai

▸ ▸ ▸ **4.** 腹八分目まで食べる
Hara hachibumme made taberu

▸ ▸ ▸ **5.** 喉が渇いた。Nodo ga kawaita

▸ ▸ ▸ **6.** チョコレートが食べたくてたまらない。
Chokorēto ga tabetakute tamaranai

▸ ▸ ▸ **7.** デザートは別腹。
Dezāto wa betsubara

Conversation at a restaurant 1

1. Excuse me.

2. Do you have an English menu?

3. Could I have one of these?

4. May I have a wet towel?

5. May I have some water?

6. Can I have more plates?

7. Could I have a fresh pair of chopsticks?

飲食店での会話1
Inshokuten deno kaiwa 1

▸ ▸ ▸ **1.** すみません。Sumimasen

▸ ▸ ▸ **2.** 英語のメニューありますか。
Ēgo no menyū arimasuka

▸ ▸ ▸ **3.** これ一つください。
Kore hitotsu kudasai

▸ ▸ ▸ **4.** おしぼりもらえますか。
Oshibori moraemasuka

▸ ▸ ▸ **5.** お水もらえますか。
Omizu moraemasuka

▸ ▸ ▸ **6.** 取り皿ください。Torizara kudasai

▸ ▸ ▸ **7.** お箸変えてください。
Ohashi kaete kudasai

Conversation at a restaurant II

1. Is there meat in this?

2. Could you hold the bacon?

3. Could you make the rice portion a little smaller, please?

4. For how many people is this?

5. My ~ still has not arrived yet.

6. Can I get this to take away?

7. Can I get the check, please?

Real dining

飲食店での会話2
Inshokuten deno kaiwa 2

▶ ▶ ▶ **1.** これ、お肉入ってますか。
Kore, oniku haittemasuka

▶ ▶ ▶ **2.** ベーコンを抜いてもらえますか。
Bēkon o nuite moraemasuka

▶ ▶ ▶ **3.** ご飯少なめにしてください。
Gohan sukunameni shitekudasai

▶ ▶ ▶ **4.** これ、何人分ですか。
Kore, nannimbun desuka

▶ ▶ ▶ **5.** まだ〜が来ていないんですが。
Mada 〜 ga kiteinain desuga

▶ ▶ ▶ **6.** これ、持ち帰りできますか。
Kore, mochikaeri dekimasuka

▶ ▶ ▶ **7.** お会計お願いします。
Okaikē onegaishimasu

リアルな食事

Conversation at a ramen restaurant

1. Extra hard noodles, please.

2. Add hot water to my soup, please (to drink the *tsukemen* soup).

3. Extra garlic, please.

4. Can I order another portion of noodles?

5. Extra large portion, please.

6. Extra bean sprouts, please.

7. Do you offer delivery?

Real dining

ラーメン屋での会話
Rāmen ya deno kaiwa

▶ ▶ ▶ **1.** バリカタで。Barikata de

▶ ▶ ▶ **2.** スープ割りください。
Sūpuwari kudasai

▶ ▶ ▶ **3.** にんにく多めで。Ninniku ōme de

▶ ▶ ▶ **4.** 替え玉お願いします。
Kaedama onegaishimasu

▶ ▶ ▶ **5.** 大盛りでお願いします。
Ōmori de onegaishimasu

▶ ▶ ▶ **6.** もやし追加で。Moyashi tsuika de

▶ ▶ ▶ **7.** 出前やってますか。
Demae yattemasuka

Conversation at an *Izakaya*

1. I'll have a draft beer to start with.

2. Cheers!

3. What are you going to have?

4. I'll pour your drink for you.

5. Your glass is empty.

6. Would you like a refill?

7. Thank you for the meal.

居酒屋での会話
Izakaya deno kaiwa

▶ ▶ ▶ **1.** とりあえず、生で。Toriaezu, namade

▶ ▶ ▶ **2.** 乾杯！Kampai

▶ ▶ ▶ **3.** 何にする？Nani ni suru

▶ ▶ ▶ **4.** おつぎします。Otsugi shimasu

▶ ▶ ▶ **5.** グラスが空いてますよ。
Gurasu ga aitemasuyo

▶ ▶ ▶ **6.** お代わりは？Okawari wa

▶ ▶ ▶ **7.** ごちそうさまでした。
Gochisō sama deshita

Food preferences

1. I don't eat meat.

2. I don't really like coriander.

3. I am allergic to eggs.

4. I am on a diet.

5. I am trying to avoid carbohydrates.

6. I am really into spicy food recently.

7. This taste is addictive.

食事の好み
Shokuji no konomi

▸ ▸ ▸ **1.** お肉は食べないんです。
Oniku wa tabenaindesu

▸ ▸ ▸ **2.** パクチーが苦手です。
Pakuchī ga nigate desu

▸ ▸ ▸ **3.** 卵アレルギーがあります。
Tamago arerugī ga arimasu

▸ ▸ ▸ **4.** ダイエット中なんです。
Daietto chū nan desu

▸ ▸ ▸ **5.** 炭水化物は控えています。
Tansuikabutsu wa hikaeteimasu

▸ ▸ ▸ **6.** 辛い物にはまってる。
Karai mono ni hamatteru

▸ ▸ ▸ **7.** この味、癖になる。
Kono aji, kuseni naru

Getting drunk

1. to get drunk ▸ ▸ ▸

2. to be wasted ▸ ▸ ▸

3. to sober up ▸ ▸ ▸

4. I am sober. ▸ ▸ ▸

5. to have a hangover ▸ ▸ ▸

6. to get tipsy ▸ ▸ ▸

7. to stagger drunkenly ▸ ▸ ▸

酔う
You

▸ ▸ ▸ **1.** 酔っ払う Yopparau

▸ ▸ ▸ **2.** ベロベロになる Berobero ni naru

▸ ▸ ▸ **3.** 酔いが覚める Yoi ga sameru

▸ ▸ ▸ **4.** シラフだよ。Shirafu dayo

▸ ▸ ▸ **5.** 二日酔いになる Futsukayoi ni naru

▸ ▸ ▸ **6.** ほろ酔い気分になる
Horoyoi kibun ni naru

▸ ▸ ▸ **7.** 千鳥足で歩く Chidoriashi de aruku

リアルな恋愛
Being in love

Encounter (dating)

1. to meet on a dating app ▸ ▸ ▸

2. to join a drinking party ▸ ▸ ▸

3. to meet by introduction ▸ ▸ ▸

4. to have a group date at a bar/restaurant ▸ ▸ ▸

5. to meet someone at work ▸ ▸ ▸

6. We were in the same grade at school. ▸ ▸ ▸

7. It was love at first sight. ▸ ▸ ▸

Being in love

出会い
Deai

▶ ▶ ▶ **1.** マッチングアプリで出会う
Macchingu apuri de deau

▶ ▶ ▶ **2.** 飲み会で合流する
Nomikai de gōryū suru

▶ ▶ ▶ **3.** 紹介で会う Shōkai de au

▶ ▶ ▶ **4.** 合コンをする Gōkon o suru

▶ ▶ ▶ **5.** 職場で会う Shokuba de au

▶ ▶ ▶ **6.** 同級生だった。Dōkyūsē datta

▶ ▶ ▶ **7.** 一目惚れした。Hitomebore shita

Impression

1. Time flies when I'm with him/her.

2. I can't keep my eyes off him/her.

3. I'm interested in him/her.

4. He/She is my type.

5. I like his/her voice.

6. I like the perfume she wears/ the cologne he wears.

7. He/She is my ideal man/ woman.

Being in love

印象
Inshō

▸ ▸ ▸ **1.** 時間が速く感じる。
Jikan ga hayaku kanjiru

▸ ▸ ▸ **2.** 目で追っちゃう。Mede occhau

▸ ▸ ▸ **3.** 気になる。Kininaru

▸ ▸ ▸ **4.** タイプ。taipu

▸ ▸ ▸ **5.** 声が好き。Koe ga suki

▸ ▸ ▸ **6.** つけてる香水が好き。
Tsuketeru kōsui ga suki

▸ ▸ ▸ **7.** 理想的。Risō teki

Progress

1. There's a chance.

2. There's no chance.

3. He/She is not replying to my LINE messages.

4. quick reply

5. not read (ignored), read (but ignored)

6. to play mind games with him/her (to make him/her like you)

7. to have a change of heart about him/her

Being in love

進展
Shinten

▶ ▶ ▶ **1.** 脈あり。Myakuari

▶ ▶ ▶ **2.** 脈なし。Myakunashi

▶ ▶ ▶ **3.** LINEが返ってこない。
Rain ga kaette konai

▶ ▶ ▶ **4.** 即レス sokuresu

▶ ▶ ▶ **5.** 未読スルー、既読スルー
Midoku surū, kidoku surū

▶ ▶ ▶ **6.** 駆け引きする Kakehiki suru

▶ ▶ ▶ **7.** 心変わりする Kokorogawari suru

リアルな恋愛

Stages of love

1. to ask for his/her contact details ▸ ▸ ▸

2. to start to like him/her ▸ ▸ ▸

3. to ask him/her on a date ▸ ▸

4. to go on a date ▸ ▸

5. to confess his/her love for him/her ▸ ▸

6. to go out with him/her ▸ ▸ ▸

7. to go on a double date ▸ ▸ ▸

Being in love

恋の段階
Koi no dankai

▶ ▶ ▶ **1.** 連絡先を聞く　Renrakusaki o kiku

▶ ▶ ▶ **2.** 好きになる　Suki ni naru

▶ ▶ ▶ **3.** デートに誘う　Dēto ni sasou

▶ ▶ ▶ **4.** デートする　Dēto suru

▶ ▶ ▶ **5.** 告白する　Kokuhaku suru

▶ ▶ ▶ **6.** 付き合う　Tsukiau

▶ ▶ ▶ **7.** ダブルデートする　Daburu dēto suru

Development I

1. to fall in love

2. to keep him/her as a backup boyfriend/girlfriend

3. one-night stand

4. to pick someone up

5. to have his/her heart broken

6. to narrow down a list of potential partners to one person

7. to weigh up his/her options (compare potential partners)

展開1
Tenkai 1

▶ ▶ ▶ **1.** 恋に落ちる　Koi ni ochiru

▶ ▶ ▶ **2.** キープする　Kīpu suru

▶ ▶ ▶ **3.** ワンナイ　Wannai

▶ ▶ ▶ **4.** ナンパする　Nampa suru

▶ ▶ ▶ **5.** 失恋する　Shitsuren suru

▶ ▶ ▶ **6.** 一人に絞る　Hitori ni shiboru

▶ ▶ ▶ **7.** 天秤にかける　Tembin ni kakeru

Development II

1. to start to dislike him/her you liked

2. to be jealous

3. to not get over him/her

4. to be still attached to him/her

5. to not be able to forget him/her

6. to cut ties with him/her

7. to recover from a broken heart

展開2
Tenkai 2

▶ ▶ ▶ **1.** 嫌いになる　Kirai ni naru

▶ ▶ ▶ **2.** ヤキモチを焼く　Yakimochi o yaku

▶ ▶ ▶ **3.** 引きずる　Hikizuru

▶ ▶ ▶ **4.** 未練たらたら　Miren taratara

▶ ▶ ▶ **5.** 忘れられない　Wasurerarenai

▶ ▶ ▶ **6.** 縁を切る　En o kiru

▶ ▶ ▶ **7.** 失恋から立ち直る
Shitsuren kara tachinaoru

リアルな恋愛

Relationship

1. to become stale

2. the person you like the most

3. one-sided love

4. mutual love

5. long-distance relationship

6. the person someone is cheating with

7. friends with benefits

Being in love

関係
Kankē

▸▸▸ **1.** マンネリ化する Mannerika suru

▸▸▸ **2.** 本命 Hommē

▸▸▸ **3.** 片思い Kataomoi

▸▸▸ **4.** 両思い Ryōomoi

▸▸▸ **5.** 遠距離恋愛／遠恋
Enkyori ren-ai/Enren

▸▸▸ **6.** 浮気相手 Uwaki aite

▸▸▸ **7.** セフレ Sefure

Relationship issues

1. to cheat

2. to get caught cheating

3. to fight with him/her

4. to change (partners)

5. to get back together

6. to two-time him/her

7. to become a dramatic and terrible situation

恋愛中のトラブル
Ren-ai chū no toraburu

▸ ▸ ▸ **1.** 浮気する　Uwaki suru

▸ ▸ ▸ **2.** 浮気がバレる　Uwaki ga bareru

▸ ▸ ▸ **3.** 喧嘩する　Kenka suru

▸ ▸ ▸ **4.** 乗り換える　Norikaeru

▸ ▸ ▸ **5.** よりを戻す　Yori o modosu

▸ ▸ ▸ **6.** 二股をかける　Futamata o kakeru

▸ ▸ ▸ **7.** 修羅場になる　Shuraba ni naru

リアルな恋愛

How to call someone I

1. ex-boyfriend/ex-girlfriend ▸ ▸ ▸

2. current boyfriend/girlfriend ▸ ▸ ▸

3. a handsome guy ▸ ▸

4. a girl who acts cute and innocent ▸ ▸ ▸

5. usually cold but sometimes affectionate ▸ ▸ ▸

6. calculating ▸ ▸ ▸

7. a person who is satisfied with his/her actual life ▸ ▸ ▸

Being in love

人の呼び方1
Hito no yobikata 1

▸▸▸ **1.** 元彼／元カノ　Motokare/Motokano

▸▸▸ **2.** 今彼／今カノ　Imakare/Imakano

▸▸▸ **3.** イケメン　Ikemen

▸▸▸ **4.** ぶりっ子　Burikko

▸▸▸ **5.** ツンデレ　Tsundere

▸▸▸ **6.** あざとい　Azatoi

▸▸▸ **7.** リア充　Riajū

How to call someone II

1. a stalker   ▸ ▸ ▸

2. losers (of society)   ▸ ▸ ▸

3. winners (of society)   ▸ ▸ ▸

4. alone   ▸ ▸

5. a person who only likes good-looking people   ▸ ▸ ▸

6. a person who is aggressive about pursuing him/her   ▸ ▸ ▸

7. a person who is calm and not aggressive about pursuing him/her   ▸ ▸ ▸

Being in love

人の呼び方2
Hito no yobikata 2

▸ ▸ ▸ **1.** ストーカー Sutōkā

▸ ▸ ▸ **2.** 負け組 Makegumi

▸ ▸ ▸ **3.** 勝ち組 Kachigumi

▸ ▸ ▸ **4.** ぼっち Bocchi

▸ ▸ ▸ **5.** 面食い Menkui

▸ ▸ ▸ **6.** 肉食 Nikushoku

▸ ▸ ▸ **7.** 草食 Sōshoku

リアルな恋愛

Separation

1. to get awkward ▸ ▸ ▸

2. to feel less in love with him/her ▸ ▸ ▸

3. for his/her eyes to wander (look at other people) ▸ ▸ ▸

4. to distant himself/herself from him/her ▸ ▸ ▸

5. for a relationship to naturally come to an end ▸ ▸ ▸

6. to reject/to break up with him/her be rejected/be broken up with by him/her ▸ ▸ ▸

7. to separate/to break up with him/her ▸ ▸ ▸

🔊 | 05-11

別れ
Wakare

▸ ▸ ▸ **1.** ギクシャクする Gikushaku suru

▸ ▸ ▸ **2.** 冷める Sameru

▸ ▸ ▸ **3.** 目移りする Meutsuri suru

▸ ▸ ▸ **4.** 距離を置く Kyori o oku

▸ ▸ ▸ **5.** 自然消滅する Shizen shōmetsu suru

▸ ▸ ▸ **6.** 振る Furu
振られる Furareru

▸ ▸ ▸ **7.** 別れる Wakareru

Onomatopoeia for love

1. My eyes met with the person I like and my heart pounded.

2. I feel frustrated from not receiving a reply.

3. I would like to cuddle/make out with my boyfriend.

4. I have a date tomorrow so I feel excited.

5. Please hold me tight.

6. Those two are very lovey-dovey.

7. When I watch a romantic film, my heart melts.

Being in love

恋愛オノマトペ
Ren-ai onomatope

▶ ▶ ▶ **1.** 好きな人と目が合ってドキドキした。
Sukina hito to mega atte dokidoki shita

▶ ▶ ▶ **2.** 返事が来なくてイライラする。
Henji ga konakute iraira suru

▶ ▶ ▶ **3.** 彼氏とイチャイチャしたい。
Kareshi to ichaicha shitai

▶ ▶ ▶ **4.** 明日はデートだからウキウキしちゃう。
Ashita wa dēto dakara ukiuki shichau

▶ ▶ ▶ **5.** ぎゅってしてー。Gyutte shitē

▶ ▶ ▶ **6.** あの二人、ラブラブだよねー。
Ano futari, raburabu dayonē

▶ ▶ ▶ **7.** 恋愛映画を見るとキュンキュンする。
Ren-ai ēga o miruto kyunkyun suru

Giving him/her a positive feeling

1. I like you.

2. Be my girlfriend/boyfriend.

3. I feel calm when I am with you.

4. I miss you.

5. I can't wait to see you.

6. I want to be with you all the time/I want to spend the rest of my life with you.

7. I've never felt this way before.

Being in love

好意を伝える
Kōi o tsutaeru

▸ ▸ ▸ **1.** 好きだよ。Suki dayo

▸ ▸ ▸ **2.** 付き合ってください。
Tsukiatte kudasai

▸ ▸ ▸ **3.** 一緒にいると落ち着く。
Issho ni iruto ochitsuku

▸ ▸ ▸ **4.** 会えなくて寂しい。Aenakute sabishī

▸ ▸ ▸ **5.** 早く会いたい。Hayaku aitai

▸ ▸ ▸ **6.** ずっと一緒にいたい。
Zutto isshoni itai

▸ ▸ ▸ **7.** こんな気持ち初めて。
Konna kimochi hajimete

Romantic rejection

1. I have feelings for someone else.

2. I have a girlfriend/boyfriend.

3. I can't see us in a romantic relationship.

4. I want to remain friends.

5. You are too good for me.

6. I don't feel like dating anyone right now.

7. You are not my type.

Being in love

告白を断る
Kokuhaku o kotowaru

▶ ▶ ▶ **1.** 他に好きな人がいる。
Hokani sukina hito ga iru

▶ ▶ ▶ **2.** 彼氏／彼女がいる。
Kareshi/kanojo ga iru

▶ ▶ ▶ **3.** 恋愛対象として見られない。
Ren-ai taishō toshite mirarenai

▶ ▶ ▶ **4.** 友達でいたい。Tomodachi de itai

▶ ▶ ▶ **5.** 自分にはもったいない。
Jibun niwa mottainai

▶ ▶ ▶ **6.** 今は誰とも付き合う気がないんだ。
Imawa daretomo tsukiau kiga nainda

▶ ▶ ▶ **7.** タイプじゃない。Taipu ja nai

Meeting someone for the first time

1. Where are you from? ▸ ▸ ▸

2. What do you do on your days off? ▸ ▸ ▸

3. What are your hobbies? ▸ ▸ ▸

4. Can I ask for your contact details? ▸ ▸ ▸

5. What's your type? ▸ ▸ ▸

6. Are you absorbed/interested in anything at the moment? ▸ ▸ ▸

7. Would you like to meet me again? ▸ ▸ ▸

Being in love

初対面
Shotaimen

▶ ▶ ▶ **1.** どこ出身ですか。
Doko shusshin desuka

▶ ▶ ▶ **2.** 休みの日は何をしていますか。
Yasuminohi wa nani o shiteimasuka

▶ ▶ ▶ **3.** 趣味はなんですか。
Shumi wa nandesuka

▶ ▶ ▶ **4.** 連絡先を聞いてもいいですか。
Renrakusaki o kītemo īdesuka

▶ ▶ ▶ **5.** どんな人がタイプですか。
Donna hito ga taipu desuka

▶ ▶ ▶ **6.** 今何かはまっているものはありますか。
Ima nanika hamatteiru mono wa arimasuka

▶ ▶ ▶ **7.** よかったらまた会いませんか。
Yokattara mata aimasenka

リアルな恋愛

Relationship status

1. single

2. unmarried

3. married

4. in a relationship

5. separated

6. engaged

7. once divorced

Being in love

交際ステータス
Kōsai sutētasu

▸ ▸ ▸ **1.** シングル Shinguru

▸ ▸ ▸ **2.** 独身 Dokushin

▸ ▸ ▸ **3.** 既婚 Kikon

▸ ▸ ▸ **4.** 交際中 Kōsai chū

▸ ▸ ▸ **5.** 別居中 Bekkyo chū

▸ ▸ ▸ **6.** 婚約中 Kon-yaku chū

▸ ▸ ▸ **7.** バツイチ Batsuichi

日本観光
Sightseeing in Japan

Asking for directions

1. I'm lost.

2. Where is ～ ?

3. Is this the right way?

4. How long will it take?

5. Can I walk there from here?

6. Can you show me on the map?

7. Are there any landmarks?

Sightseeing in Japan

道を聞く
Michi o kiku

▶ ▶ ▶ **1.** 道に迷いました。
Michi ni mayoimashita

▶ ▶ ▶ **2.** ～はどこですか。~ wa dokodesuka

▶ ▶ ▶ **3.** この道で合ってますか。
Kono michi de attemasuka

▶ ▶ ▶ **4.** どのくらいかかりますか。
Donokurai kakarimasuka

▶ ▶ ▶ **5.** ここからそこに歩いて行けますか。
Kokokara soko ni aruite ikemasuka

▶ ▶ ▶ **6.** 地図で教えてください。
Chizu de oshiete kudasai

▶ ▶ ▶ **7.** 目印はありますか。
Mejirushi wa arimasuka

Using trains and buses

1. Which train line should I take?

2. Does this train go to ～ ?

3. Where should I change trains?

4. Where can I buy a train ticket?

5. Is there a bus stop nearby?

6. What time is the last train?

7. I lost my ticket.

Sightseeing in Japan

電車やバスに乗る
Densha ya basu ni noru

▶ ▶ ▶ **1.** 何線に乗ればいいですか。
Nani sen ni noreba īdesuka

▶ ▶ ▶ **2.** この電車は〜へ行きますか。
Kono densha wa 〜 e ikimasuka

▶ ▶ ▶ **3.** どこで乗り換えればいいですか。
Doko de norikaereba īdesuka

▶ ▶ ▶ **4.** 電車の切符はどこで買えますか。
Densha no kippu wa doko de kaemasuka

▶ ▶ ▶ **5.** この近くにバス停はありますか。
Kono chikaku ni basutē wa arimasuka

▶ ▶ ▶ **6.** 終電は何時ですか。
Shūden wa nanji desuka

▶ ▶ ▶ **7.** 切符をなくしてしまいました。
Kippu o nakushite shimaimashita

Getting in a taxi

1. Where is the taxi stand?

2. I would like to go to ～ .

3. The address is at ～ .

4. Turn at that corner.

5. I'm in a rush, so could you please drive faster?

6. Please stop here.

7. How many minutes will it take?

タクシーに乗る
Takushī ni noru

▶ ▶ ▶ **1.** タクシー乗り場はどこですか。
Takushī noriba wa dokodesuka

▶ ▶ ▶ **2.** ～までお願いします。
～ made onegaishimasu

▶ ▶ ▶ **3.** 住所は～です。Jūsho wa ～ desu

▶ ▶ ▶ **4.** そこの角を曲がってください。
Sokono kado o magatte kudasai

▶ ▶ ▶ **5.** 時間がないので急いでもらえますか。
Jikan ga nainode isoide moraemasuka

▶ ▶ ▶ **6.** ここで止まってください。/ここでお願いします。
Kokode tomatte kudasai/Kokode onegaishimasu

▶ ▶ ▶ **7.** 何分くらいかかりますか。
Nampun kurai kakarimasuka

Conversation at a hotel 1

1. I'd like to check in please.

2. May I change the room to a non-smoking room?

3. What time is the meal (dinner)?

4. What time is checkout?

5. Can I leave my luggage here?

6. I'd like a wake-up call at 7 am.

7. Which floor is the public bath?

ホテル1
Hoteru 1

▶ ▶ ▶ **1.** チェックインをお願いします。
Chekku in o onegaishimasu

▶ ▶ ▶ **2.** 禁煙の部屋に変えられますか。
Kin-en no heya ni kaeraremasuka

▶ ▶ ▶ **3.** 食事は何時ですか。
Shokuji wa nanji desuka

▶ ▶ ▶ **4.** チェックアウトは何時ですか。
Chekkuauto wa nanji desuka

▶ ▶ ▶ **5.** 荷物はここに預けられますか。
Nimotsu wa koko ni azukeraremasuka

▶ ▶ ▶ **6.** 7時にモーニングコールをお願いします。
Shichiji ni mōningu kōru o onegaishimasu

▶ ▶ ▶ **7.** 大浴場は何階にありますか。
Daiyokujō wa nankai ni arimasuka

Conversation at a hotel II

1. Are there any tourist attractions nearby?

2. I'd like to call a taxi, please.

3. Where is the nearest station?

4. Can I exchange money?

5. Is there anywhere nearby where I can eat ~ ?

6. I would like to order room service.

7. I would like to check out.

ホテル２
Hoteru 2

▶ ▶ ▶ **1.** 近くに観光名所はありますか。
Chikaku ni kankō mēsho wa arimasuka

▶ ▶ ▶ **2.** タクシーをお願いします。
Takushī o onegaishimasu

▶ ▶ ▶ **3.** 一番近い駅はどこですか。
Ichiban chikai eki wa dokodesuka

▶ ▶ ▶ **4.** 両替はできますか。
Ryōgae wa dekimasuka

▶ ▶ ▶ **5.** 近くに〜が食べられるお店はありますか。
Chikakuni ~ga taberareru omise wa arimasuka

▶ ▶ ▶ **6.** ルームサービスを頼みたいんですが。
Rūmusābisu o tanomitaindesuga

▶ ▶ ▶ **7.** チェックアウトをお願いします。
Chekkuauto o onegaishimasu

Trouble at a hotel

1. There is no hot water. ▸ ▸ ▸

2. I can't connect to the Wi-Fi. ▸ ▸ ▸

3. I left my key in the room. ▸ ▸ ▸

4. The air-conditioner is not working. ▸ ▸ ▸

5. The toilet is not flushing. ▸ ▸ ▸

6. I would like to change my room. ▸ ▸ ▸

7. May I change my dinner reservation time? ▸ ▸ ▸

Sightseeing in Japan

ホテルのトラブル
Hoteru no toraburu

▸ ▸ ▸ **1.** お湯が出ません。Oyu ga demasen

▸ ▸ ▸ **2.** Wi-fiがつながりません。
Waifai ga tsunagarimasen

▸ ▸ ▸ **3.** 部屋に鍵を置いて出てしまいました。
Heya ni kagi o oite deteshimaimashita

▸ ▸ ▸ **4.** エアコンが利きません。
Eakon ga kikimasen

▸ ▸ ▸ **5.** トイレが流れません。
Toire ga nagaremasen

▸ ▸ ▸ **6.** 部屋を変えてください。
Heya o kaete kudasai

▸ ▸ ▸ **7.** 夕飯の時間を変えてもらえますか。
Yūhan no jikan o kaete moraemasuka

Travel plans

1. I need to book a Shinkansen ticket.

2. I want to climb Mt. Fuji.

3. I want to eat *Takoyaki* in Osaka.

4. I want to stay in an old-fashioned *ryokan*.

5. Let's wear Yukata (Kimono).

6. I hope I can make Japanese friends.

7. I asked a person for a guided tour on the Internet.

Sightseeing in Japan

旅の計画
Tabi no kēkaku

▶ ▶ ▶ **1.** 新幹線を予約しなきゃ。
Shinkansen o yoyaku shinakya

▶ ▶ ▶ **2.** 富士山に登ってみたい。
Fujisan ni nobotte mitai

▶ ▶ ▶ **3.** 大阪でたこ焼きを食べたい。
Ōsaka de takoyaki o tabetai

▶ ▶ ▶ **4.** 昔ながらの旅館に泊まりたい。
Mukashinagara no ryokan ni tomaritai

▶ ▶ ▶ **5.** 浴衣（着物）を着ようよ。
Yukata(kimono) o kiyōyo

▶ ▶ ▶ **6.** 日本人の友達ができたらな。
Nihonjin no tomodachi ga dekitarana

▶ ▶ ▶ **7.** ネットで観光案内を頼んだよ。
Netto de kankō annai o tanondayo

Real opinions while traveling I

1. There are too many people in Tokyo.

2. It's quite busy in Kyoto during spring.

3. There are many fashionable people in Harajuku, aren't there?

4. People in Osaka are friendly.

5. All Japanese people seem busy.

6. We can't go to all the places in one day.

7. I have to go to ～ next time.

旅のリアルな感想1
Tabi no riaruna kansō 1

▶ ▶ ▶ **1.** 東京って人が多すぎ。
Tōkyōtte hito ga ōsugi

▶ ▶ ▶ **2.** 春の京都は混んでるね。
Haru no kyōto wa konderune

▶ ▶ ▶ **3.** 原宿っておしゃれな子多くない？
Harajukutte osharena ko ōkunai

▶ ▶ ▶ **4.** 大阪の人ってフレンドリー。
Ōsaka no hitotte furendorī

▶ ▶ ▶ **5.** 日本人ってみんな忙しそう。
Nihonjintte minna isogashisō

▶ ▶ ▶ **6.** 1日じゃ回りきれない。
Ichinichi ja mawarikirenai

▶ ▶ ▶ **7.** 次は絶対〜に行きたい。
Tsugi wa zettai 〜 ni ikitai

Real opinions while traveling II

1. This place is a little pricy, isn't it? Prices are steep in Japan.

2. Japanese food is amazing!

3. The Japanese *ryokan* was just okay.

4. The outdoor *onsen* (bath) felt so good.

5. The level of customer service is amazing.

6. I don't really like sushi.

7. I want to come here again.

Sightseeing in Japan

旅のリアルな感想2
Tabi no riaruna kansō 2

▶ ▶ ▶ **1.** この店、ちょっと高くない？ 日本って物価高いね。
Kono mise, chotto takakunai Nihontte bukka takaine

▶ ▶ ▶ **2.** 日本料理って最高！
Nihon ryōritte saikō

▶ ▶ ▶ **3.** 旅館はまあまあだったね。
Ryokan wa māmā dattane

▶ ▶ ▶ **4.** 露天風呂が気持ちよかった！
Roten buro ga kimochi yokatta

▶ ▶ ▶ **5.** 接客のレベル高すぎ。
Sekkyaku no reberu takasugi

▶ ▶ ▶ **6.** 寿司は苦手かも。
Sushi wa nigate kamo

▶ ▶ ▶ **7.** また来たいねー。 Mata kitainē

Buying souvenirs

1. What are the local specialties here?

2. I am looking for ~ .

3. What is this?

4. Can you go any cheaper?

5. I like this color. (while pointing at a product)

6. I will take this.

7. How much is it in total?

Sightseeing in Japan

お土産を買う
Omiyage o kau

▶ ▶ ▶ **1.** ここの名物は何ですか。
Koko no mēbutsu wa nandesuka

▶ ▶ ▶ **2.** ～を探しています。
～ o sagashiteimasu

▶ ▶ ▶ **3.** これは何ですか。Kore wa nandesuka

▶ ▶ ▶ **4.** 安くなりませんかね。
Yasuku narimasen kane

▶ ▶ ▶ **5.** この色がいいです。Kono iro ga īdesu

▶ ▶ ▶ **6.** これにします。Kore ni shimasu

▶ ▶ ▶ **7.** 合計でいくらですか。
Gōkē de ikura desuka

Going to the police

1. Are there any police stations nearby?

2. I dropped my wallet.

3. I picked up a credit card.

4. My bicycle was stolen.

5. I would like to ask for directions.

6. I don't have much time.

7. I don't need a (financial) reward.

警察に行く
Kēsatsu ni iku

▸ ▸ ▸ **1.** この近くに交番はありますか。
Kono chikaku ni kōban wa arimasuka

▸ ▸ ▸ **2.** 財布を落としてしまいました。
Saifu o otoshite shimaimashita

▸ ▸ ▸ **3.** クレジットカードを拾いました。
Kurejitto kādo o hiroimashita

▸ ▸ ▸ **4.** 自転車を盗まれました。
Jitensha o nusumaremashita

▸ ▸ ▸ **5.** 道を聞きたいんですが。
Michi o kikitaindesuga

▸ ▸ ▸ **6.** あまり時間がありません。
Amari jikan ga arimasen

▸ ▸ ▸ **7.** お礼は要りません。Orē wa irimasen

日本観光

Conversation when meeting someone for the first time

1. Would you be able to take a photo for me?

2. May I take a photo?

3. Thank you so much for being kind to me.

4. Are you from here?/ Are you a local?

5. I can only speak a little bit of Japanese.

6. Do you speak English?

7. Where are you from?

Sightseeing in Japan

出会った人との会話
Deatta hito tono kaiwa

▸ ▸ ▸ **1.** 写真を撮っていただけませんか。
Shashin o totte itadakemasenka

▸ ▸ ▸ **2.** 写真を撮ってもいいですか。
Shashin o tottemo īdesuka

▸ ▸ ▸ **3.** 親切にしていただいてありがとうございます。
Shinsetsu ni shite itadaite arigatō gozaimasu

▸ ▸ ▸ **4.** 地元の方ですか。
Jimoto no katadesuka

▸ ▸ ▸ **5.** 日本語は少ししか話せないんです。
Nihongo wa sukoshi shika hanasenaindesu

▸ ▸ ▸ **6.** 英語を話しますか。
Ēgo o hanashimasuka

▸ ▸ ▸ **7.** どこから来たんですか。
Dokokara kitandesuka

Useful phrases

1. Is there anyone who can speak English?

2. I'm just looking.

3. Can I use a credit card?

4. Excuse me, please let me through.

5. Could you speak more slowly, please?

6. Please say that again.

7. Do you have Wi-Fi here?

Sightseeing in Japan

便利フレーズ
Benri furēzu

▶ ▶ ▶ **1.** 英語が話せる人はいますか。
Ēgo ga hanaseru hito wa imasuka

▶ ▶ ▶ **2.** 見てるだけです。Miteru dake desu

▶ ▶ ▶ **3.** カードは使えますか。
Kādo wa tsukaemasuka

▶ ▶ ▶ **4.** すみません、通してください。
Sumimasen, tōshite kudasai

▶ ▶ ▶ **5.** ゆっくり話していただけますか。
Yukkuri hanashite itadakemasuka

▶ ▶ ▶ **6.** もう一度言ってください。
Mōichido itte kudasai

▶ ▶ ▶ **7.** Wi-Fiありますか。Waifai arimasuka

note

note

Valiant Japanese Language School
ヴァリアント ジャパニーズ ランゲージ スクール

Valiant Japanese Language School in Roppongi was established with the aim of teaching practical Japanese used in daily life. The lessons, which teach practical expressions rooted in real-life Japanese conversation, have been well received by many and are gaining in popularity. The school has over 140,000 followers on Instagram.

日常生活で本当に必要になる、 リアルな日本語を教えることを目的として設立された六本木の日本語学校。 日本の実生活での会話に根づいたリアルな表現を教えるレッスンが好評で、 人気を集めている。 学校が運営するインスタグラムはフォロワー数14万を超える。

デザイン　dig
イラスト　あわい
音声収録　ELEC
校正　鷗来堂
DTP　山口 良二
執筆協力　三輪 正寿、 金井 由衣、 Grant Campbell

SUPER REAL JAPANESE
スーパー　リアル　ジャパニーズ

2023年 3 月10日　初版発行
2024年 8 月30日　5 版発行

著者／Valiant Japanese Language School
ヴァリアント　ジャパニーズ　ランゲージ　スクール

発行者／山下 直久

発行／株式会社KADOKAWA
〒102-8177　東京都千代田区富士見2-13-3
電話　0570-002-301 (ナビダイヤル)

印刷所／TOPPANクロレ株式会社

●お問い合わせ
https://www.kadokawa.co.jp/ (「お問い合わせ」へお進みください)
※内容によっては、お答えできない場合があります。
※サポートは日本国内のみとさせていただきます。
※Japanese text only

定価はカバーに表示してあります。